12/20/2

MArshA,

All you Need is

Him

God Bless,
Much Love,
Henrietta Burnett

Him

HEALING INSPIRATIONAL
MESSAGES FOR DAILY LIVING

MARCIA GETHERS

purposely
created
PUBLISHING

HIM

Published by Purposely Created Publishing Group™
Copyright © 2020 Marcia Gethers

Printed in the United States of America
ISBN: 978-1-64484-270-6

Special discounts are available on bulk quantity purchases by book clubs, associations and special interest groups. For details email: sales@publishyourgift.com or call (888) 949-6228. For information log on to www.PublishYourGift.com

WELCOME TO SERENITY

If you can find the time and place to soak your mind with quietness, oh, how sweet it could be! How relaxing it can be if we could find such a place where there are no interruptions. It would be a place of refuge where you can draw back from the everyday concerns of the world and breathe freely. It would be a place where you would not have to figure out how to handle everything yourself.

Does a place like this really exist? Is there such a place where you don't have to carry heavy weights of responsibility? I believe there is such a place where everyday concerns can be as light as a feather. This place only exists in the presence of God. When you seek His presence and peace as your refuge, He will carry your cares for you. He tells us we can cast our cares on Him (1 Peter 5:7). In other words, let Him do the fixing. If we allow Him to fix our lives, we will not have to worry about breaking down. No load is too heavy for Him to carry. He has strong arms of love, peace, wisdom, joy, and strength. He will carry whatever you need Him to carry, so that you can have His peace that surpasses and goes beyond your understanding (Philippians 4:7).

Take time to feel His presence and sing songs of praise and melodies in your heart. Think on the good things, the blessings, how He takes care of you and your family. You may not have everything you want; however, He makes what you have be just enough. He keeps your mind when things get chaotic. Just when you think you have had enough, you find strength to go one more step. Did you know that strength comes from Him? He is strong enough to carry the load. So, why in our weakness would we try to carry such a heavy load? We have someone who is capable of working for us. There is no greater strength than that of Jesus. The beauty is that He has enough to give to everyone equally. We need only to ask Him.

Table of Contents

Introduction

The contents of this book show how thoughts and circumstances affect our emotional and spiritual development. It is designed to reach a diverse range of people from all walks of life and environments and show the benefit of applying scripture to their lives. It holds no claim for professional counseling but offers spiritual encouragement through faith. In my weakest moments, I have found turning to God and reading His Word were my only means for refreshment and my push to get past dark places where I thought no light would shine again.

No matter who you are or what title you hold, you will encounter situations that you just cannot manage alone. When you try in your own strength to fix situations that are entirely too heavy to carry and when you have exhausted all your finite human frailties, that is when you can have the opportunity to experience the infinite greater power of God. God has given us His Word to face our challenges and to become victorious over them. By applying His Word to your life, you can have a changed mindset of hope, boldness, and confidence. To understand how to apply God's Word, you must have a personal relationship with Him through faith and absolute trust and confidence that He will provide everything you need. If you desire this relationship, why not simply pray and believe.

Lord, I want You to be Lord over my life. I trust You to forgive my sins, those shortcomings that separate me from You. I open my heart to You by faith. Thank You, Jesus. Amen.

God has the ability to strengthen you. It is my desire to provide hope and show the extent of God's love for us. He did not promise that we would not suffer or bad things would not happen; however, He promised that He would strengthen us through them all. We are more than conquerors through Him, and nothing can separate us from His love (Romans 8:37-38). Just take one day at a time.

Hope

What is hope, or how do you define hope as it pertains to your specific challenges and what you face in life? For some, it is a word or state of being that does not exist. It is a vague fog, an uncertainty. When one thinks of hope, it is looking toward the future. Whether it means the next minute, hour, day, week, or year, it is the future. It is a change in time that we will not see again.

The anticipation of hope can sometimes be overwhelming. The thought of what will happen if what you hoped for does not become reality can be mind-boggling. In life, we face disappointments, failures, hurt, pain, detachments from love ones—the list goes on. If you put your hope in people alone, the outcome can be disheartening. I submit to you that true hope has to come from an understanding far beyond our mind. It has to come from a source greater than any finite entity. That greater entity is God, Jesus Christ, who is our only hope. You must put your entire trust and faith (which is a form of hope) in God, knowing that He has all the power and that He is our hope. He is the one who can do exceedingly, abundantly above all we can ever think or imagine (Ephesians 3:20).

Hope goes beyond our minds and into our inner beings. The thought of having no hope is like standing at an iron door and wanting to get in. We try with all our might and strength to pull that door open, but we cannot. We do not notice that the key is right there in a plant sitting nearby. We are too focused on trying to knock down the door in our own strength; obviously, we need some assistance to get through. In reality, if we use the key that has already been provided, we can enter the door. If we could only realize that the key would awaken us to the beauty of life, we would pick it up. Jesus is that key. However, fearing it will be a waste of time; we will not give it a second look. First looks are important. That is how God wants us to see Him. He wants us to see Him first as important, significant. He is right there, everpresent. We need only to look with our hearts and not with our finite minds. God is infinite. There is no ending to His presence. His presence is one of beauty, grace, refreshment, security, and undying hope.

Whatever you hope for, you can trust God to give you the solace you need. It may not be what you thought it would be; however, it will be what you need. He certainly knows what is best for you at all times.

Reach out to God and allow Him to be the anchor of hope that holds you.

"He leads me beside quiet waters, He restores my soul. He guides me in the paths of righteousness for His name sake" (Psalm 23:2b-3, NASB).

Morning Prayer

Order my steps, O great Jehovah. Whether big or small, I will walk in the right direction as I follow You. There may be detours along the way, and my footing may get crooked, and the road may be dusty at times; however, I trust You to blow away the dust and clear my path, so that I may see my way to walk on the straight path You have set before me.

STRENGTH AND COMFORT

Valleys

There may be valleys wherein we find ourselves at times; however, deliverance is before you. You do not have to climb what seems like a mountain of obstacles; simply lift your hands in total surrender. God is able to move that mountain. He will send His chief angel to war for you, so you may accomplish all He has for you to do, big or small. While in valleys, fear can easily put you at a standstill. Satan often uses various temptations to get you to turn away from God and not believe God's Word. Knowing and obeying God's Word is an effective weapon against temptation. Jesus, Himself, was tempted by Satan; however, Jesus stood on the truth and power of God's Word (Luke 4:2). When you reflect on the tool of the Word, it can help you move out of your valley. You will know that God's presence is your place of safety.

"Do not fear For I am with you" (Isaiah 41:10a, NASB).

"For in Him we live and move and have our being" (Acts 17:28).

"God is our refuge and strength, a very present help in trouble" (Psalm 46:1).

"The Lord is my light and my salvation; whom shall I fear: the Lord is the strength of my life; of whom shall I be afraid?" (Psalm 27:1).

"Finally, be strong in the Lord, and in the strength of His might" (Ephesians 6:10, NASB).

Feeling Overwhelmed

When you feel like throwing in the towel, God is there to dry your tears. Our heavenly Father knows all and does everything according to His will. When we look to Him, we will see clearly that everything is in order.

Your particular challenge may be different from someone else's. Remember the attention you give it determines how much power it will have over you. Whatever God allows in our lives, He knows we are able to endure it.

Temptation happens to everyone, so don't feel you are alone. Recognize those things that give you trouble. Pray for God's help. Seek friends who have faith to connect with your faith.

"No temptation has seized you except what is common to man, and God is faithful; he will not let you be tempted beyond what you can bear. But when you are tempted, he will also provide a way out so that you can stand up under it"
(1 Corinthians 10:13, NIV).

Weakness Made Strong

Feeling a little weak? God tells us, "Be strong and courageous, do not be afraid, or tremble, for the Lord your God is the one who goes with you. He will not fail you or forsake you" (Deuteronomy 31:6, NASB).

Sometimes we just want to run away and hide. Life gets so tough, and it feels like we are carrying the weight of the world on our shoulders. It seems like everyone is depending on us to be a rescue engine.

When you run out of fuel, that is when you say, "Lord, I cannot drive this train any longer, and I need You to be the conductor. You are my tunnel, so that I may reach the bright light at the end." When tears fill your eyes and darkness engulfs you, rest your mind in Him and know that a brighter day is coming.

"Weeping may endure for a night, but joy cometh in the morning" (Psalm 30:5).

Don't Worry (Grieving)

Your heart may be heavy because I have departed,
Don't worry, don't frown, and please don't be down
for it is for heaven I am bound,
Yes, I have gone on to receive my glorious crown
Although my time with you may seem
short, just remember the good fight I truly fought
I must leave you to take my rest,
For unto my Father I have given my best.
So now, you must carry out the work I left.
Let Christ rise up in you, presenting
yourself mighty and bold,
As you diligently bring in the lost souls.
One day again your face I will see, then you will also
know what it is to be fully free.
So, don't worry, don't frown, and please don't be
down, for one day, you too will receive your crown.

God's Comforting Hand

There is no pain God is not able to heal

All that we can ever think or feel,

Remember God knows and He cares.

You can talk to Him, even cry out,

He is sure to listen without a doubt.

When you are finished, He always has the answer

He will tell you which way to go,

While letting nothing but unconditional love flow.

He is so sweet and gentle,

Your sorrowful heart He will touch.

He will mend it completely,

Everything you will ever need,

He will give you freely.

Only trust and believe!

Let the warmth of God's love flow in you

Healing and comforting you as only His love can do.

Prayer of Help

Lord, help me to focus on You. Fix my mind and heart that I may rest in You. I believe You will provide whatever provisions I need for what I am facing. I trust You as I walk in faith and let go of anything that refutes Your promises. Surely, You shall show Yourself strong on my behalf.

God cause me to see in the Spirit what cannot be seen in the natural.

"For the eyes of the Lord run to and fro throughout the whole earth, to shew himself strong on the behalf of them whose heart is perfect" (2 Chronicles 16:9).

"Thy Word is a lamp unto my feet, and a light unto my path" (Psalm 119:105).

What you cannot see, God can. Keep looking in His Word to be enlightened.

THANKFULNESS

A Heart of Thanksgiving

Today, Lord, I can see, I can feel, and I can think. I have a portion of good health, and I am breathing; therefore, I shall not complain.

T – Teach me O Lord to hear Your voice

H – Help me to find my way

A – All I have, to Thee I owe

N – Needing You more every day

K – Keep me strong when trials come to weaken

S – Songs of Zion I sing unto You daily

G – Give me a pure and loving heart

I – Inspire me to press on

V – Ventilate my mind with Your thoughts

I – In You I live, move, and have my being

N – Nearer to Thee, I want to be

G – Grant me Your peace, for great is Thy faithfulness

Life Is Beautiful

Life's simple pleasures are all we need
In order to enjoy our brief stay here.
Listening to the peaceful sounds of nature,
That God has graciously supplied.
Oh to be at peace, nothing overpowering you!
Knowing in spite of it all, God will bring you through.
Be truly thankful for this life,
That Jesus paid for with His stripes.

My Joy

The joy of the Lord is my strength.

No matter what, I will rejoice.

He has given me new life.

In His presence, I find complete joy

I say again, no matter what, I will rejoice.

For He has given me new life.

I love the Lord because He first loved me.

When I cried unto the Lord, He heard me.

He healed my wounded heart and my sin sick soul.

What a mighty good God He is.

He gives me strength from day to day,

To face whatever may come my way.

Oh blessed is the name of the Lord!

He gives laughter when there should be tears.

He gives mercy where there should be judgment

He carries me through the storms of life,

I don't know what I would do without Him.

He is always there.

Therefore, I will trust in the Lord until I die.

A New Day

Sometimes we just need to affirm ourselves.

This is a glorious day. It is a day I have never seen before. This day has been ordained especially for me. I'm anointed to do great things.

There are so many possibilities for me.

I will soar high, think big as I breathe in the fresh newness of this day.

As I embrace this day, I will experience new excitement, adventure, and prosperity of every kind.

Another day wiser, another day stronger, and another day more confident—yes that's me.

This is my day, and I will enjoy it to the fullest.

Declare His Praise

As you sing from the depths of your heart, it does not matter the tune. Jesus makes the notes sweet music to His ears.

Therefore, "make a joyful noise unto the Lord all ye lands. Serve the Lord with gladness; come before his presence with singing" (Psalm 100:1-2).

"He only is my rock and my salvation; He is my defense; I shall not be moved" (Psalm 62:2).

With thanksgiving in your heart greatly rejoice in him!

"Rejoice in the Lord always, again, I say rejoice" (Philippians 4:4, NASB).

HIS GREATNESS

God's Grace Is Sufficient

God's grace is sufficient over our lives for whatever situation or challenge we face in life, and His hand of mercy is forever upon us.

As we reflect on all the provisions He gives for our daily needs, it makes our struggles become tolerable.

When we learn to be content in whatever state we find ourselves, we can appreciate the small graces He gives and not take them for granted.

If you have water to wash your face and suddenly it's turned off for a day, when it comes back on, you are so happy and realize what a small thing, yet I took it for granted.

GRACE:
GENTLE; REFRESHING; ABUNDANT;
CARING; EMBRACE

Make It Personal

The Lord is my Shepherd who protects, covers, and watches over me. I am one of His sheep that grazes in His pasture. I lie down in peace, and do not worry, as He provides still waters that rush through me and brings calmness.

Restoration is available as He restores my mind, my heart, and my soul. I am His righteousness. I am privileged, special, loved, forgiven, and made complete. I stand in a place of honor because He is my Daddy. He withholds nothing from me. He guides me and helps me make right decisions.

Although I may go through dark valleys, He walks with me through all my disappointments, heartaches, and setbacks. I will fear no evil because I trust Him. He uses His rod, the Word, as His hands to protect and fight for me.

He comforts me and assures me that everything will be okay. He showers me with abundant blessings in the presence of my enemies.

With the oil of anointing poured upon my head, I possess extraordinary power from the Holy Spirit.

Surely, His goodness and mercy is sufficient for me, and He shall be with me all the days of my life, and I shall dwell with Him forever.

ENCOURAGE YOURSELF

Me and Only Me

Be yourself—the person God created you to be. Allow Him to develop His character and gifts in you, so that He can use you personally for His glory.

Be established and complete in who you are.

Trust God and know that He accepts you for who you are. Although in the eyes of others, you may appear imperfect, know that God sees you as perfect.

"Who shall also confirm you to the end, that ye may be blameless in the day of our Lord Jesus Christ"
(1 Corinthians 1:8).

Christ alone holds the true meaning of life because Christ is life, there is no need to seek God by means of rituals.

I Am Who I Am

I am who I am because this is who God has created me to be.

All my talents, my inconsistencies, and my shortcomings come with who God has created me to be.

I stand unique and small, a woman of many pieces, all being shaped, and formed together like clay into the masterpiece, that God has created me to be.

Sometimes I am up,

Sometimes I am down,

Sometimes I don't understand,

God, just what is your plan?

But wait! I see a vision; it's becoming clearer,

I am no longer small.

I have grown tall in my character, bold in my confidence.

I am as strong as a tree planted by the sea,

Although, the waves of life blow, I shall not be moved!

For when God is finished with me

I will be the complete woman,

He has created me to be.

Yes, I am who I am!

"Man Up"

He is God's first creation.
He is who God formed from the dust of the land with
His mighty hands.
Within him is power,
The very breath of God is his soul.
He is strong in stature, character, and wisdom
The expressed image of God
God created man to lead and to guide,
He also made woman from a rib out of his side.
A man speaks with wisdom and dignity,
and is called to be the head and not the tail.
Therefore, my brothers follow God.
Let God teach, develop, and deliver you.
Let Him shape, mold, and build you from within,
ultimately let Him set you free.
Then shall you take a stand, beginning at home,
and then expanding throughout the land
Let everyone know that you do make a difference,
For you are a rare piece of art.
A Real Man

STAND STRONG

Trials and Tests

Sometimes we may feel as though our lives are at a standstill. At every turn, there seems to be disappointments, uncertainties, decisions, and responsibilities. Something is always being added to the pile.

As the pile continues to grow, a wall develops. We can't seem to get through it or go around it. Tired and worn, we sit upon this wall to take a rest. After a while, there appears a crack, and if we are not careful, everything seems to crumble . . . Therefore,

"Let us hold fast the profession of our faith without wavering, for He is faithful that promised"
(Hebrews 10:23).

Work Out - Fit to Endure

Exercise your faith when you are facing persecution and pressure. Do not faint or give up. This is the time to persevere. During times of great stress, you can feel God's presence more closely and find help you never thought possible if you turn to Him. Show Him your faith is real by standing and enduring.

"We are troubled on every side, yet not distressed; we are perplexed, but not in despair. Persecuted, but not forsaken, cast down, but not destroyed"
(2 Corinthians 4:8).

We may think we are at the end of our rope; however, there is always hope. God is with us and will never abandon us. All our setbacks, humiliation, and trials are opportunities for Christ to demonstrate His power and presence in us.

He says, "Ye are of God little children and have overcome them; because greater is he that is in you, than he that is in the world" (1 John 4:4).

"In the world ye shall have tribulation; but be of good cheer, I have overcome the world" (John 16:33b).

Conquering Uncertainties

"The Lord is thy keeper: the Lord is thy shade upon thy right hand. The Lord shall preserve thy going out and thy coming in from this time forth and even evermore" (Psalm 121:5, 8).

Oftentimes, we face situations where we cannot see the outcome with our natural eyes. We are sometimes in unfamiliar surroundings, and we want to run away. However, if God has spoken to you, then you must obey Him without question and believe that He will perform what He said.

"Trust in the Lord with all thine heart and lean not unto thine own understanding; in all thy ways acknowledge Him and He will direct thy path" (Proverbs 3:5-6).

Watching You

God is watching from afar. He knows your situation, your challenges. He is watching and waiting to see if you will give it to Him.

Regardless of the inevitable struggles you face, you are not alone. If you can remember that the ultimate victory has already been won, you can claim the peace of Christ in your troublesome times. God is a shelter when we are afraid. He is our Protector and will carry us through the dangers and fears of life. Trust Him no matter how intense your fears may be.

Resist the temptations that cause you to get discouraged. Stand strong and believe. Refuse to allow fear to undermine your faith or your ability to achieve and maintain emotional and mental stability. "The breakthrough that will follow this time of testing will be well worth the effort necessary to overcome," says the Lord. **Do not fear –**

"Fear thou not; for I am with thee; be not dismayed, for I am thy God. I will strengthen thee; yea, I will help thee; yea, I will uphold thee with the right hand of My righteousness" (Isaiah 41:10).

SERENITY

A Special Place

The Lord said, "Behold there is a place by Me, and thou shall stand upon the rock, and it shall come to pass, while My glory passeth by, that I will put thee in a cleft of the rock, and will cover thee with My hand while I pass by" (Exodus 33:21-22).

"My glory is upon you. I assure you that you will continue to overcome. Tenderly and endearing love shines through you. I give you hope as I keep you in the cleft of my arms. All My qualities I impart to you. You are a beautiful blessing, my child."

Personal Encounter

When you are broken, open your heart and experience God's presence, love, and faithfulness. Let the warmth of His presence engulf you like a cloak. May He be like a spring of fresh water gently pouring over you, refreshing and quenching your every thirst. Drink in deeply.

He Hears

No matter where we find ourselves and even in the darkest part of life when we feel down or disheartened, God is there. He is with you. He covers you with His love and protection. Even before you were born, while in your mother's womb, He fashioned you and made you just the way He wanted you to be. He laid His mighty hands upon you. He, therefore, can guide and direct you. He can take that crooked part of us and make it straight. God already knows everything we may say or begin to utter. He is very familiar with our ways, desires, wants, and shortcomings. He understands us as no one else does. He knows how we feel even while we are going through. There is no hiding from Him.

JESUS - The Restorer of Life!

Walk Peacefully with Jesus

Sometimes, we wonder how we will cope with everything or do all that is expected of us. We go through each day sometimes mentally rehearsing how we will fit it all in.

God wants us to train our minds, discipline ourselves and our actions to hear His voice and trust in Him. He wants us to be aware of the provisions He has given us, so we can move smoothly and confidently through what we face.

The provision He has given us is peace in Jesus the Christ. He said,

"My Presence shall go with thee, and I will give thee rest" (Exodus 33:14).

God has already given us peace; we just need to draw upon it.

"My peace I give to you, not as the world gives do I give you" (John 14:27, NASB).

THE ALMIGHTY

Jesus

I truly love Jesus
A few years ago, I met Him
He ushered me into His presence
He told me of His love for me
and how He will always be there for me

He told me that He would guide me
That He would comfort me
That He would give me peace
That He would give me wisdom
Everything I would ever need,
He promised He would provide.

Oh, He walks with me during the day
and talks with me along the way
At night, He lays me down,
He rocks me in His arms until I am asleep,
Then early in the morning
He awakens me with His gentle touch,
He breathes fresh new life into my soul.

Such love is indescribable!
There is no love like Jesus' love
and guess what?
He told me that it would be for all eternity.
Jesus, You are my ALMIGHTY love

The Greatest Gift

Jesus, the Redeemer, the Savior gave the greatest gift—eternal life
He humbled Himself as no one else could ever do,
and took on the sins of the world to die for you and me
They hung Him high and stretched Him wide, they also pierced Him in His side.
It was the darkest day ever when He yelled out a deadly cry
Why? Why? Why?
However, Jesus already knew He was giving life light for the world to see.
We are no longer slaves to sin and death,
Jesus paid for us with His life when He rose from the dead, Hallelujah He is alive for evermore.
This is a time of liberation,
For the gift of eternal life that was given
The shed blood on Calvary's cross declares
IT IS FINISHED!

He Is Risen

They laid Him in an empty cave that many thought to
be His grave.
The guards stood by to secure as they were told, not
realizing the blessing that would soon unfold.
The entrance was sealed tight,
While close watch was kept overnight,
However, in the morning, oh what a sight
He is gone they begin to say,
Someone has come and taken him away
They begin to tremble with fear
As they ran hurriedly to tell a lie,
Because telling the truth, they would surely die.
The rulers begin to question,
Where, oh where can He be,
He could not have set Himself free.
The guards replied in disbelief
How He disappeared we did not see.
No one was there where Jesus once laid,
He had risen from the grave
Our sin debt He had FULLY paid.
Oh death where is your sting?

Him

For my Lord Jesus is most powerful

Over anything you can bring.

Yes, Jesus is LORD and SAVIOR and He is KING!

Proclaim your victory, declare your freedom, and

Receive your deliverance,

HE IS RISEN, HE IS RISEN, HE IS RISEN!

Jesus Dropped the Charges

The case has been heard
The verdict is in
The testimonies have been shared, the evidence
presented
Persecution is all around,
The jury is set,
Oh, how bleak it looks,
Everything is about to end,
But wait!
My attorney (Master Jesus) they have not met,
He steps down from His throne,
Stands in the gap.
He replies,
I have reviewed from afar
From the time you entered into this world,
The penalty has been paid in full
No balance is due,
For my Son Jesus has fully represented you.
His credentials are eternal,
He has never lost a case,
Therefore the charges have been dropped,

Today you are set FREE!

"There is therefore now, no condemnation in Christ Jesus" (Romans 8:1).

The Word Speaks

Prayers are our communication to God. However, in our prayers we must know that whatever we cry out for we can find the answer in His Word. Our job is to listen and receive with our hearts what He says. Perhaps you may not know what to pray; however, you can see He already knows. If you feel weak, troubled, need encouragement, or just want to know who He is, draw from the Word

"Hear. O Lord, when I cry with my voice, have mercy also upon me, and answer me" (Psalm 27:7).

"God is our refuge and strength, a very present help in trouble" (Psalm 46:1).

"He giveth power to the faint: and to them that have no might he increaseth strength (Isaiah 40:29).

"But they that wait upon the Lord shall renew their strength; they shall mount up with wings as eagles; they shall run, and not be weary; and they shall walk, and not faint" (Isaiah 40:31).

"The Lord is my light and my salvation; whom shall I fear: the Lord is the strength of my life; of whom shall I be afraid?" (Psalm 27:1).

"Wait on the Lord; be of good courage, and he shall strengthen thine heart wait, I say, on the Lord" (Psalm 27:14).

"For I know the thoughts that I think toward you, saith the Lord, thoughts of peace, and not evil, to give you an expected end" (Jeremiah 29:11).

"Call unto me, and I will answer thee and show thee great and mighty things, which thou knowest not" (Jeremiah 33:3).

"Behold, I am the Lord, the God of all flesh; Is there anything too hard for me?" (Jeremiah 32:27).

Winning the Race

"The Lord God is my strength, and he will make my feet like hinds' feet, and he will make me to walk upon mine high places" (Habakkuk 3:19).

God will give His followers surefooted confidence through difficult times. They will run like deer across rough and dangerous terrain. At the proper time, God will bring about His justice. In the meantime, God's people need to live in the strength of His Spirit, confident in His ultimate victory over the difficulties we face. We cannot see all that God is doing, and we cannot see all that God will do, but we can be assured that He is God and will do what is right.

Have confidence: "Cast not away therefore your confidence, which hath great recompense of reward" (Hebrews 10:35).

Hold your head up, walk proud, keep pressing through with the inner power from deep within your soul. Allow the Holy Spirit to work in you.

LOVE, LOVE, LOVE

The Importance of Love

God calls us to love even when we don't want to. It is not based on how we feel; it has everything to do with His unconditional love for us. If He can love us regardless of how much we turn our backs on Him, then why can't we extend a little love? Love suffers long. God's love demonstrates patience with imperfect people. His love does not envy - shows real love. His love does not parade itself, does not put on a big show in order to impress others.

In John 15:12, Jesus said the two greatest commandments are that we love Him and love one another as He has loved us.

Jesus is the ultimate example of love. The sacrifice He made by His death on Calvary points to true love. His sacrifice shows that love is more than a feeling... it is action. Jesus says in John 13:35, the way people will know that we belong to Him and are His disciples (followers) is if we have love for one another.

Love Basics

God's reason for creating the world is love. His love for us is unconditional. Nothing we do can take God's love from us. When we demonstrate a life motivated by love, it is well pleasing to God. Love involves humility, sacrifice, forgiveness, kindness, and endurance. Here is what God says about love.

"Love is patient, love is kind. It does not envy, it does not boast, it is not proud. It is not rude, it is not self-seeking. It is not easily angered, it keeps no record of wrongs. Love does not delight in evil but rejoices with the truth. It always protects, always trust, always hopes, always perseveres. Love never fails"
(1 Corinthians 13:4-8, New International Version).

Agape Love

God wants to teach us this kind of love.

Agape means an undefeatable and unconquerable goodwill that always seeks the highest good of another person...no matter what he does. It is a self-giving love that gives freely without asking anything in return. It is choosing to let the Holy Spirit love through us.

We must submit to God, lay aside our personal desires and wants, and not allow our "flesh" to decide for us. In other words, do not be dependent upon our moods, attitudes, or feelings but draw from the Holy Spirit.

God's supernatural love in our hearts is a work in progress.

Our Heavenly Daddy

The love our Heavenly Daddy gives is embedded
deep in our hearts, our minds, and our spirits.
A bountiful blessing you shall forever reap.
Always encouraging, and ever so wise
With each day, He brings something new
He gives of Himself so kind and free
Whenever you feel you cannot pass life's test
Think of His encouraging words, which will inspire
you to press.
PROTECTOR, CONFIDANT, HERO,
A loving daddy who watches over you
One who allows mistakes
While teaching you the value of life
While showing you how special you are.
Our Heavenly Daddy has His mighty hand upon us
He is hiding us in the cleft of the rock
We are never alone
Remember, He sent Jesus to take care of us
We can talk to Jesus, even cry out
He is sure to listen without a doubt
He will always have the answer
and will tell you which way to go.

Majestic Love

God's love for you is so majestic and unwavering
It matters not what you face in life, He is able to carry
you, to keep, and to see you through.
So, do not be dismayed by what has occurred,
Know that in God's sight, you are special and there is
no one else like you.
You are fearfully and wonderfully made.
God has a purpose for your life that only you can fulfill
So, wait on the Lord, be of good courage and He will
strengthen you.
Reach out and grab hold of His love.

Love That Never Fails

Christ's love is far greater than all else on earth. His love is never ending. He always cares. When we do not understand, we can still know He is there.

His love is not fickle, we are all loved the same.

He came to give us salvation

His love gives correction

His love gives forgiveness to all who will ask

He will help with that task

His love gives us strength to get through each day

His love gives us sweet rest on the weary way

With His love we overcome addiction's mighty grip

His miraculous love rips Satan's strong hold

His love gives perfect peace when our trials increase.

His love brings us real joy

His Word is our feast

His love calms our fears when by faith we believe

His precious promises are ours to receive

His love is perfect

He makes no mistakes.

God says, "Be calm and rest your heart and mind in Me."

FORGIVENESS AND FAITH

Forgiveness

Forgiveness, like love, is a pre-requisite for your relationship with God and others. If we search our hearts, we might find that there might be a little unforgiveness about something that has occurred in our lives. We have not let go of these things which hinder our ability to truly receive love. Unforgiveness affects our relationship with God. It cuts off our communication with Him and robs us of so many things. Therefore, we cannot have faith. The Word says if we regard iniquity in our hearts, God will not hear our prayers (Psalm 66:18).

Faith

Faith is total dependence on God and a willingness to do His will. It is complete and humble obedience to God and the readiness to do whatever He calls us to do. It is important to have the right kind of faith, faith in our all-powerful God.

"For without faith it is impossible to please Him, for he that cometh to God must believe that He is and that He is a rewarder of them that diligently seek Him" (Hebrews 11:6).

God assures us that all who honestly seek Him and those who act in faith on the knowledge of God they possess shall be rewarded. Your reward is His love and peace.

Belief is necessary for God to move in your situation. The beginning point of faith is believing who God is and then believing He will do what He says.

Oftentimes, we face situations and cannot see the outcome with the natural eye. We are sometimes in unfamiliar surroundings, and we want to run away. However, if God has spoken to you, then you must obey Him without question and believe that He will perform what He said.

Faith builds the thing you hope for in the realm you cannot see.

God gives you a fresh, new revelation of Himself through your faith. He chooses you, then He calls you, then He shapes your life into an intimate, loving relationship with Him. God waits for you to agree with Him. When you agree, He begins to unfold what He has called you to do. He allows you to come to a place spiritually where He shows you that He is almighty and nothing is impossible for Him.

A mind that waivers is not completely convinced that God's way is best. It vacillates between feelings, the world's ideas, and God's commands. If your faith is new, weak, or struggling, remember God is trustworthy; be loyal to Him. To stabilize your wavering or doubtful mind, commit yourself wholeheartedly to God.

A Little Confidence

Knowing what God says in His Word will help you to believe that your situation can change and get better.

"Trust in the Lord with all thine heart and lean not unto thine own understanding; in all thy ways acknowledge Him and He will direct thy path" (Proverbs 3:5-6).

"For the Lord shall be thy confidence, and shall keep thy foot from being taken" (Proverbs 3:26).

"Receive my instruction, and not silver; and knowledge rather than choice gold" (Proverbs 8:10).

"For ye shall go out with joy, and be led forth with peace; the mountains and the hills shall break forth before you into singing, and all the trees of the field shall clap their hands" (Isaiah 55:12).

"Lift up your heads, O ye gates; and be ye lift up, ye everlasting doors; and the King of glory shall come in" (Psalm 24:7).

"The Lord is thy keeper: the Lord is thy shade upon thy right hand. The Lord shall preserve thy going out and thy coming in from this time forth and even evermore" (Psalm 121:5-8).

"So shall my word that goeth forth out of my mouth, it shall not return unto me void, but it shall accomplish that which I please, and it shall prosper in the thing whereto I sent it" (Isaiah 55:11).

Often, we cannot see immediate results from following God. When we are not certain what to do, reading scriptures is a sure step we can take to give us clarity.

Make an effort each day to read and think about God's Word. Stand on what you know God has said, and you will reap the benefits of obedience.

No Need to Doubt

We wonder how we will cope with everything or all that is expected of us. We go through each day sometimes mentally rehearsing how we will do this or that. God wants us to train our minds and discipline ourselves in our actions to hear His voice and trust in Him. He wants us to be aware of the provisions He has given us to move smoothly and confidently through what we face. The provision He has given us is peace in Jesus the Christ.

"And He said, My Presence shall go with thee, and I will give the rest" (Exodus 33:14). Imagine God as a friend walking with you. Like a friend, you feel free to talk, share your hearts desires, and you listen. You are so focused on this special intimate time together that you let go of your distractions and worries. This moment becomes everything to you. Walking peacefully with Jesus means you connect with His will and change your thoughts to His.

God has already given us peace; we just need to draw upon it.

"Peace I leave with you" (John 14:27a, NASB).

SERVITUDE

I Pledge My Allegiance to God

I pledge my allegiance to the one, true, living God, Jesus Christ.

Who for me on the cross gave His life that I might live.

In Him is truth, justice, and righteousness

He reins conquering death, hell, and the grave!

He has risen unto life eternal.

There is no other God who is

Savior, Master, and Lord

Jesus the Christ is the giver of life, liberty, and freedom.

I pledge my allegiance to Him, once and for all.

Amen!

Lord, Help My Unbelief

When we become desperate, when our backs are against the wall, we then have to become radical in our actions. Everything looks bleak. Nothing is going right. Society and circumstances tell us there is no way we will get through this; it is impossible.

We worry about what people will think; however, we have to be willing to take a risk and step out on faith regardless of how it may look. We cannot stay in the same old mindset, or we will die, maybe not literally, but our ability to make something happen will dwindle away. We have to move, or we will lose. We must be willing to press. How bad do you want things to change? Change is necessary for progress; it is inevitable. We need to be confident in Christ in the most unbelievable situations, and then move from confidence to expectation. Expect God to move on your behalf because of the promises He has made to you. Be willing to trust God in situations and places where you have never been before.

We cannot be stuck in the "what if." We can't keep looking back, but we have to have a forward gaze, eyes fixed on the prize, or we will miss our connection to hook up to the next level of grace and blessings. We cannot carry the trash of disbelief, disappointment, despair, or drudgery; it's too heavy. Our bags are too full; therefore, we cannot put on the new confidence, the new strength, the new knowledge that God has for us. Know that God promises are sure. We must watch carefully where we walk or take up residence. We must make our steps firm and in the direction that God leads and not our associates. Remember that some people do not want you to move on; they want to keep you in a stagnated position because they know they cannot go with you. They will not be able to latch on to you and live off your blessings. Watch out for the vision killers. God says, "I will go before you and make the crooked places straight. I will break in pieces the gates of brass and cut in sunder the bars of iron" (Isaiah 45:2, NASB).

In other words, God has already cleared everything out; all we have to do is walk in it.

Now, how hard is that? God's Word is simple and pure, but we make it so complicated, trying to analyze everything. What we need is childlike faith and just go! God says, "Don't worry; just pray and believe."

So, tell yourself, I know my healing and my peace are coming!

Thank You, Jesus; the victory is mine!

Yet I'll Still Praise My God

With all that is happening, all the pressures, all the disappointments, I'll still praise my God for He is worthy to be praised.

Praise God because He created you. Praise God for His mercy. Praise God for His love. Praise God because He has already determined what's best for you. Encourage yourself.

"For I know that all things work together for good to them that love God, to them who are the called according to His purpose" (Romans 8:28).

I cannot see it with the natural eye, but I know God is working it all out, and we have the victory.

"Lift up your heads, O ye gates; and be ye lift up, ye everlasting doors; and the King of glory shall come in. Who is this King of glory? The Lord strong and mighty, the Lord mighty in battle" (Psalms 24:7-8).

I Turned It Over to the Lord

That problem that I had,
I turned it over to the Lord,
and guess what, He worked it out.
So, can I stand to be blessed? I would say yes
For I know that the blessing is already here.
The Lord is keeping me; He is holding me
He is lifting me above all the pressures.
Thank You, Lord for being my everything
You are so true to Your Word. You promised You
would never leave me nor forsake me.
You promised, No good thing will You withhold from
them that walk upright and will give me the desires
of my heart.

Thank you for rocking me in your arms,
For hiding me in the cleft of the Rock,
THE SOLID ROCK, JESUS
Oh, I can see the storms passing over,
I stand ready and waiting to receive my blessings. I
shall praise You, magnify You, and esteem You high.
Oh, how I adore You! Your MAJESTY is ever so
beautiful.

PERSEVERANCE

The Process

The process may come in different ways depending on the individual. However, it is necessary for God to develop us.

Oftentimes, this may call for giving up friends, a particular lifestyle, or changing our surroundings. It most assuredly involves spending time studying God's Word and praying and applying what we read to our lives. Our goal should be to know Him and not to allow anyone or anything to take our eyes off that goal.

We are not perfect. There may be a lot that needs fixing in us. Let us not be too concerned about the way we once were or what happened in the past. Why not move forward to a new beginning? Seek to be who God intended us to be. No matter how difficult it may appear, if we press, we can obtain whatever it is we are seeking to accomplish. Always remember we can learn from our struggles.

It's Only a Test

There is another test before you. What do you do? Just jump over the hurdle. Believe that God has given you hind's feet.

God will never leave you nor forsake you. There is nothing too hard for God.

"Do not fear or be dismayed because of this great multitude, for the battle is not yours but God's" (2 Chronicles 20:15, NASB).

"You need not fight in this battle; station yourselves stand and see the salvation of the Lord on your behalf, O Judah and Jerusalem; Do not fear or be dismayed, tomorrow go out to face them, for the Lord is with you" (2 Chronicles 20:17, NASB).

Maybe you are in a situation right now and you think you will be defeated. I say to you this battle can only be won with God's spiritual sword, which is His Word.

Therefore, put your trust in God.

Let Him take care of this battle; you may be in a race but remember with Jesus you shall cross the finish line to victory.

Amen!

Be Assured

God will give His people the confidence needed in difficult times. It may be rough, and sometimes we may encounter dangerous surroundings; however, at the proper time, God will send help. For now, live in the strength of His Spirit and faith. Be confident that you have the victory over the challenges you face.

"Cast not away therefore your confidence, which hath great recompense of reward" (Hebrews 10:35).

Do not stop believing your deliverance is coming. Hold your head up, walk proud, and keep pressing through with the inner power from deep within your soul, allowing the Holy Spirit to work in you.

Your Blessing

"Blessed is the man that walketh not in the counsel of the ungodly but his delight is in the law of the Lord" (Psalm 1:1a, 2a, NASB).

Abide in Him

Seek Him concerning everything

Fellowship with Him

Study His Word

Walk in newness of life

Love your neighbor

Let go of unforgiveness

Stand and be a witness

Worship Him in spirit and in truth

The Finish Line

"The Lord God is my Strength and He will make my feet like hinds' feet, and He will make me to walk upon mine high places" (Habakkuk 3:19a).

Like a deer running across a field and into a road of danger, your feet shall be made swift that you might escape to freedom.

Keep running until you see the finish line of safety.

Keep pressing through with the inner power from deep within your soul.

Freedom

I Am Free
I am free as free can be,
Because of the new life
God has given me.
Yes, the chains are broken,
The bondage has lifted
No longer do I walk
With my head hung down,
God has anointed me with His crown.
The great seal of approval has
Been placed upon my life,
There is no longer misery or strife.
I walk and I step high,
No longer swaying from side to side
Which way do I go?
Which way do I choose?
Is not a question for me!
God directs me to His path,
Not crooked, not wide,
But simply long and straight
The only way to His heavenly gate

I Surrender

Lord, I surrender all to You. With my mind, heart, and body, I long to rest in You. I tried to do it alone, but I realize I cannot do anything without You. I ask You to remove the fear, the cloudy thoughts in my mind, the hurt, unforgiveness in my heart, and the weakness in my body. I stretch my hands to You. My arms are open wide to receive Your guidance, Your strength, Your love, and Your peace. I need You, O Lord, truly I do. Touch me with Your hands of mercy. I surrender, I surrender, I surrender all. Amen.

.

IN HIS TIME

A Time for Everything

"Not as though I had already obtained it or have already become perfect, but I press on so that I may lay hold of that for which also I was laid hold of (for me) by Christ Jesus" (Philippians 3:12, NASB).

You may not have it yet, but know if you press on, and forget about your setbacks, you will reach the prize. What is the prize? It is the plan Jesus has for your life.

Lay aside anything harmful and forsake anything that may distract you from being an effective Christian.

Read God's Word, pray, and change your way of thinking. Ask God to make an inner change in you, so what's on the inside will reflect on the outside.

This will take some time...There is a time for everything. God will perfect that which concerns you; however, it does not come easy. We must go through the process of Him refining us. He will let you know when your transformation is complete.

There will be tears, struggles, uncertainties, and standing alone, but in due season, when it is your time to blossom, when He moves you into the place of victory, you will see that it was all for your good. You will become stronger, wiser, and have a deeper level of faith and love for Christ.

Hear Me O God

Deliver me, O God, from all that would oppress me and bring me shame and sorrow.

Lord, help me to be strong in this situation.

Dear God, lead me according to Your will.

Open my eyes, Lord, that I might see You.

I lift my face to You, O God. You are my help.

O Lord, I ask for wisdom and courage.

I am weary, God. Please fill me with Holy Spirit energy.

Draw me nearer to You, Lord Jesus.

Fill my heart with Your compassion, O Lord.

Lord, let Your love pour over me like rain.

I choose to follow You in all my ways.

W L W L

WATCH with your spiritual eyes. That the eyes of your understanding may be enlightened.

LISTEN for the voice of God – He speaks. My peace I leave with you, not as the world gives you.
Most of the time, we wonder how we will cope with all that we face or what is expected of us. We go through each day sometimes mentally rehearsing how we will do everything.

WAIT for the Holy Spirit's instructions. He is our teacher. "In quietness and confidence will be your strength" (Isaiah 30:15b).

While you are waiting, continue to pray, "God order my steps. Help me to know Your voice. Give me understanding of Your Word. Make me to know that I am engulfed with Your presence. Grow me up in You, Lord. Teach me how to exercise Your patience, walk in Your grace and Your mercy. I need You, Lord; I cannot make it on my own. You are my strength. You are my peace. I trust You, Lord."

LEARN from what you experienced.

God is telling us do not worry about it. I got you, so rest in Me. Take the load off. Do not think about it or ponder on the thing.

"Thou wilt keep (you) in perfect peace, whose mind is stayed on thee, because he trusteth in thee"
(Isaiah 26:3).

God wants to train our minds and discipline us in our actions to hear His voice and trust Him. He wants us to be aware of the provisions He has given us in order to move smoothly and confidently through all we face. The provision He gave is Jesus the Christ.

"He that dwelleth in the secret place of the Most
High shall abide under the shadow of the Almighty"
(Psalm 91:1).

God is our covering. He is hovering over us. He is our refuge and fortress.

God is our firm foundation when the cares of life try to penetrate us so deeply. If we concentrate on the Holy Spirit abiding in us as a shining light, the darkness of our circumstances will simply fade.

God designed us to depend on Him. As our Shepherd, He watches over us and carries us as sheep to safety when we get confused or lose our way. We must follow the instructions He has given us for life... the Bible.

FULL COVERAGE
PROTECTION

Soldiers, Put on Your Armor

For every battle we face, we need a strategy to win. In fighting that battle, our equipment must be strong enough to penetrate our opponent's attempts. We must know how to use our weapons and be focused on the task before us and not be distracted by wavering thoughts.

> *For the weapons of our warfare are not carnal, but mighty through God to the pulling down of strong holds; Casting down imaginations, and every high thing that exalted itself against the knowledge of God, and bringing into captivity every thought to the obedience of Christ;" (2 Corinthians 10:4-5).*

Change your thought pattern to what you have read in God's Word.

Recognize that the enemy is trying to control you and fill your mind with falsehoods. He has been trying to disrupt your emotions. At one time, we may have fallen for his untruths; however, now is the time to escape the strongholds that the devil used to grip you. Today, confess that you are turning to God. Submit every thought to the Holy Spirit. Ask Him for help to learn to use the weapons of warfare that He has given.

Darkness Has No Power

God covers us with His light, love, and protection.

He can dispel darkness and things unseen to the natural eye that are visible in the spirit. Anything you may think or say is impossible, God already knows the possibility. He understands us as no one else does. He knows how we feel even while we are going through and even while fumbling in darkness. There is no hiding from Him.

God purpose my words. Make them sweet and refreshing to You and others. Impart love, patience, joy, and peace. Open my eyes, remove the veil of darkness, and develop my character that it may be that of Christ's-likeness shining bright in a dark world.

No Room for Bondage

Do not allow the enemy to hold you in bondage!

He tries to hold us captive by getting us to think that we are not loved or by keeping us from realizing our self-worth and how beautiful we are to God from the inside out. We have to continue to stand on the Word of God and know that we are fearfully and wonderfully made (Psalm 139:14). God knows all we think and what we face. Once we give it to Him, leave it with Him, and trust Him to handle it, we will be set free in every area of our lives. So, daily say to God, "You, Lord, have given me a sound mind not the spirit of fear; You, Lord, love me unconditionally. I will not allow the enemy to hold me in the past, but I am moving forward in You to receive all that You have for me."

We have mighty weapons of prayer and praise that we must use even when we do not feel like it. Even when we feel we are alone and others have abandoned us, we must remember that God is always there. If we can just "muster" up a "Thank You" or "hallelujah," it will cause the enemy to flee. The more we call on Him and believe that He is with us, the more powerful we become. Then we will gain momentum, strength, and our eyes will be opened to see how truly special we are to God.

Take time out for yourself, love yourself, appreciate yourself, and the rest will come to pass. For it is in Him that we are made complete. Amen!

A Vessel for the Master's Use

We are as fragile clay jars containing great treasure. We have experienced many things that have caused cracks in our lives; however, God wants to fix the cracks.

"We are pressed on every side by troubles, but we are not crushed. We are perplexed, but not driven to despair. We are hunted down, but never abandoned by God. We get knocked down, but we are not destroyed" (2 Corinthians 4:8-9, NLT).

We will face many things in life, and sometimes those things may grip us so tightly that it seems as though our very breath is squeezed out of us or as if we are hyperventilating. However, there is good news; God has supplied us with the greatest oxygen, which is His blood. It runs through our bodies and removes all of the "clots" that try to cause us to hyperventilate. The blood of Jesus is powerful enough to flow through the clots, the blockages, and the wounds and will allow us to breathe easy through our challenges.

We are vessels in the Potter's hand. We have been marred, bruised, and discarded at times. There is a big crack and if we take one more hit, we will break into many pieces. Be encouraged. Know that God is ready to pick up all the pieces and remake us.

"And the vessel that he made of clay was marred in the hands of the potter, so he made it again another vessel" (Jeremiah 18:4).

God is the Potter who puts us on the wheel of life, and He keeps shaping us and molding us until He fashions us into a vessel fit for His use. He takes those things that we think will destroy us and makes them become pillars of strength. He wants to fix us, mend relationships, reconstruct that which is torn down, and stir up the gifts in us. We are in the master Potter's hands.

"For ye have need of patience, after you have done the will of God, ye shall receive the promise" (Hebrews 10:36).

Just be patient!

Prayer

"May God grant you according to the riches of His glory, to be strengthened with power through His son Jesus. May the Holy Spirit dwell in your heart by faith; and that you being rooted and grounded in love, may be able to comprehend with all the saints what is the breadth and length and height and depth and to know the love of Christ which surpasses knowledge, that you may be filled with all the fullness of God" (Ephesians 3:16-19, NASB).

Lord, I pray that You tear down any hindrances and allow me to walk free of every attempted trap the enemy has devised for my destruction for the rest of my life. In Jesus' name I pray, Amen.

Abide Totally in Christ

"He that dwelleth in the secret place of the most High shall abide under the shadow of the Almighty. I will say of the Lord, He is my refuge and my fortress; my God; in him will I trust. Surely, he shall deliver thee from the snare of the fowler, and from the noisome pestilence. He shall cover thee with his feathers, and under his wings shall thou trust; his truth shall be thy shield and buckler. Thou shalt not be afraid for the terror by night; nor for the arrow that flieth by day. Nor for the pestilence that walketh in darkness; nor for the destruction that wasteth at noonday. A thousand shall fall at thy side, and ten thousand at thy right hand; but it shall not come nigh thee"
(Psalm 91:1-7).

In whatever troubles we face, we can run to God as our safe place. God is our protector. We may not see Him and may feel He's left us in our hard situations, but His protection is real. He does not forget us. Stay in His presence by standing on His Word, praying, and giving your cares to Him. Do not be overcome by fear. Remember we cannot do it alone.

Only Believe

Believe Jesus is God's Son.

"Whosoever shall confess that Jesus is the Son of God, God dwelleth in him and he in God" (1 John 4:15).

Receive Him as Savior and Lord.

"But as many as received Him to them gave he power to become the sons of God, even to them that believe on his name" (John 1:12).

Do what God says.

"And he that keepeth His commandments dwelleth in him, and he in him. And hereby we know that He abideth in us, by the Spirit which he hath given us" (1 John 3:24).

"This is my commandment. That ye love one another, as I have loved you" (John 15:12).

Ask God to help you solve your problems or give you strength to endure them. Then be patient. God will not leave you alone with your problems; He will stay close by and help you grow.

"And these things write we unto you, that your joy may be full" (1 John 1:4).

Completion, release, joy, peace, is only made possible by a living relationship with Christ.

Sometimes, we may feel like we are in prison hiding from our circumstances, caught in despair and fear. We may feel like we are unable to pull ourselves out. It is at these times that we must call on the Lord.

"Bring my soul out of prison, that I may praise thy name" (Psalm 142:7a).

Receive Him as Savior and Lord

"But you must continue in the things which you have learned and been assured of, knowing from whom you have learned them" (2 Timothy 3:14, New King James Version).

"Blessed is the man that walketh not in the counsel of the ungodly but his delight is in the law of the Lord" (Psalm 1:1a, 2a).

Lord, thank you for speaking to me. I hear, and I am revived.

Him Inspired

Thanks to my Lord and Savior Jesus Christ who through my trials and life tragedies imparted His love, faith, hope, knowledge, and strength to write this book. I give Him all praise, honor, and glory. For it was through the many dark valleys, reading, praying, and believing His Word, I now experience victory, joy, and the tenacity to stand and declare to others that they can also.

Special thanks to my mentor Patricia Johnson-Harris for introducing me to Purposely Created Publishing Group. Your expertise and warm words of encouragement were the push I needed to start the process of submitting my manuscript. I really appreciate your kindness and commitment to me during this time.

To everyone who purchased this book, I pray you were uplifted by His Words.

God Bless You!

Reference Scriptures

Psalm 23:2-3

Habakkuk 3:19

Isaiah 30:15

John 15:12

Acts 17:28

John 13:35

Psalm 46:1

1 Corinthians 13

Psalm 27:1, 14

Psalm 139:14

Ephesians 6:10

Psalm 66:18

1 Corinthians 10:13

Hebrews 11: 6, 8

Deuteronomy 31:6

Proverbs 3:5-6

Psalm 30:5

Proverbs 8:10

2 Chronicles 16:9

Philippians 3:12, 13

Psalm 119:105

Psalm 24:7, 8

1 Corinthians 1:8-9

Romans 8:28

Colossians 2:10

Psalm 24:7, 8

Hebrews 10:23, 35, 36

Psalm 1

Psalm 121:5, 8

1 Peter 5:7

Proverbs 3:5, 6

2 Corinthians 2:16

2 Corinthians 4:8

Philippians 2:5

1 John 4:4, 15

Ephesians 3:16, 19

John 16:33

John 3:24

Exodus 33, 14, 21, 22

John 1:4

John 14:27

Psalm 142:7

Psalm 28:7

Psalm 46:1

Psalm 91

Isaiah 40:29, 31

Isaiah 41:10

Isaiah 55:11, 12

Jeremiah 29:11

Jeremiah 33:3

Jeremiah 32:27

2 Chronicles 20:15, 17

About the Author

Marcia Gethers is an author and inspirational speaker whose holistic approach to restoring and empowering people sets her apart. She believes that people who are ordinary to the world are extraordinary to God.

She is the author of *Triumphantly Winning: From Pain to Power* and *Power in the Enemy's Camp: Overcoming Tragedy to Triumph.* Her purpose is to encourage people to trust God for hope and love during perilous times. Over the past fifteen years, she has been the keynote speaker at numerous conferences in Baltimore and the surrounding areas.

Her passions are taking care of people, promoting healthy lifestyles for people experiencing mental, social, physical, and economic challenges, serving youths and the homeless, and spreading the gospel.

In her spare time, she enjoys walking, visiting historical sites, and listening to music. She is married to Minister Rickey Gethers and is extremely proud of her grandson, Nijiere.

To connect, email her at
marciapower32@gmail.com

CREATING DISTINCTIVE BOOKS
WITH INTENTIONAL RESULTS

We're a collaborative group of creative masterminds
with a mission to produce high-quality books to position
you for monumental success in the marketplace.

Our professional team of writers, editors, designers,
and marketing strategists work closely together to ensure
that every detail of your book is a clear representation
of the message in your writing.

Want to know more?
Write to us at info@publishyourgift.com
or call (888) 949-6228

Discover great books, exclusive offers, and more at
www.PublishYourGift.com

Connect with us on social media

@publishyourgift

CPSIA information can be obtained
at www.ICGtesting.com
Printed in the USA
FSHW020211041020
74331FS

9 781644 842706